Dad Can Cook

by Ellen Dalton

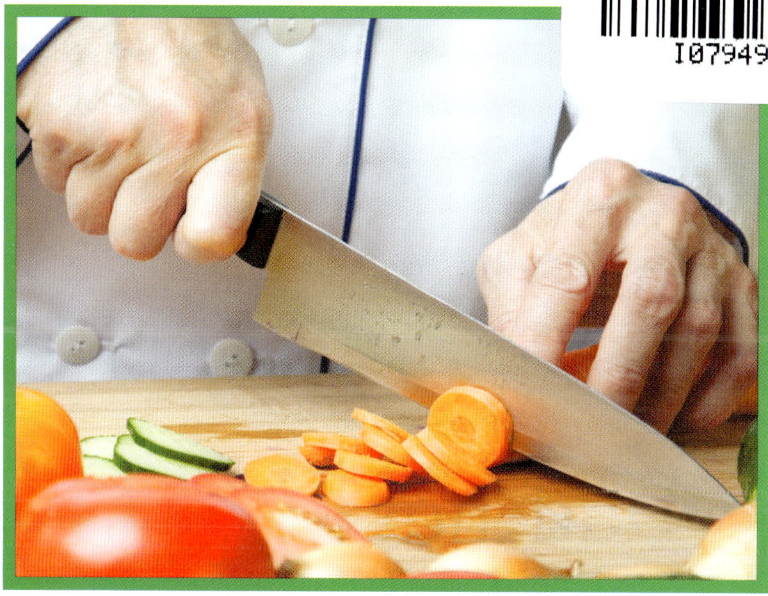

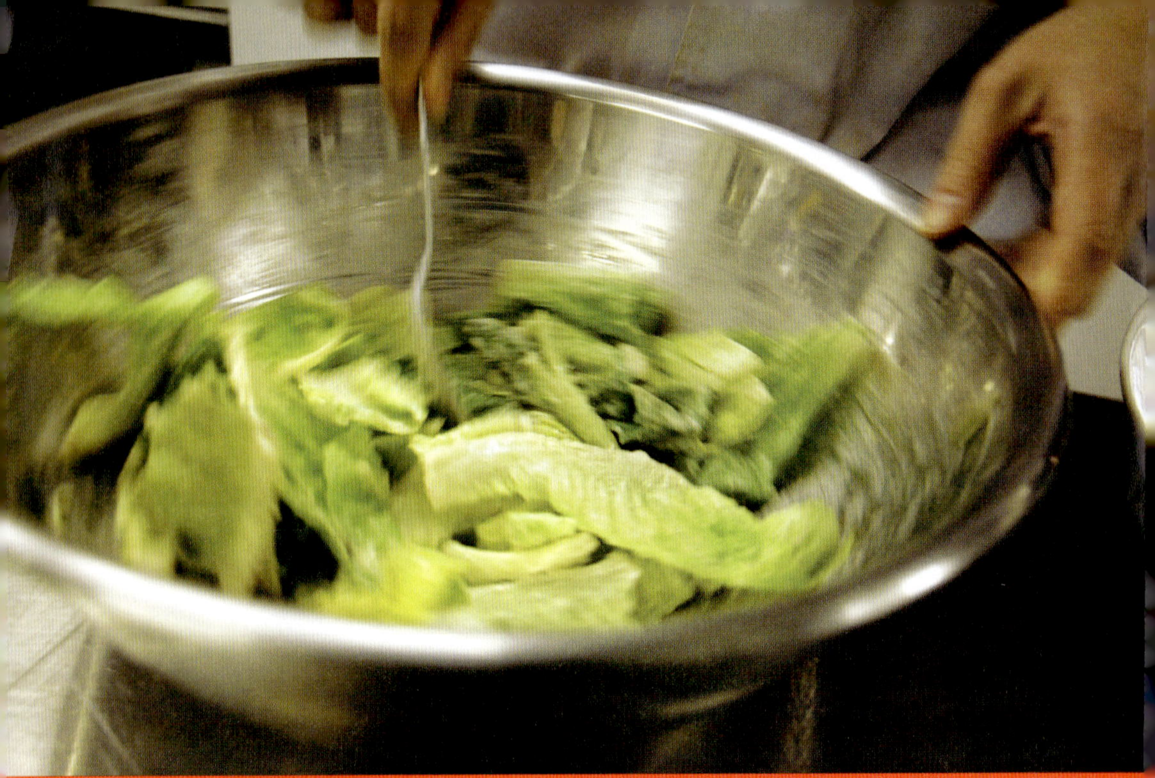

Dad has a 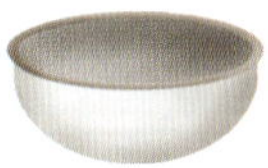 bowl .

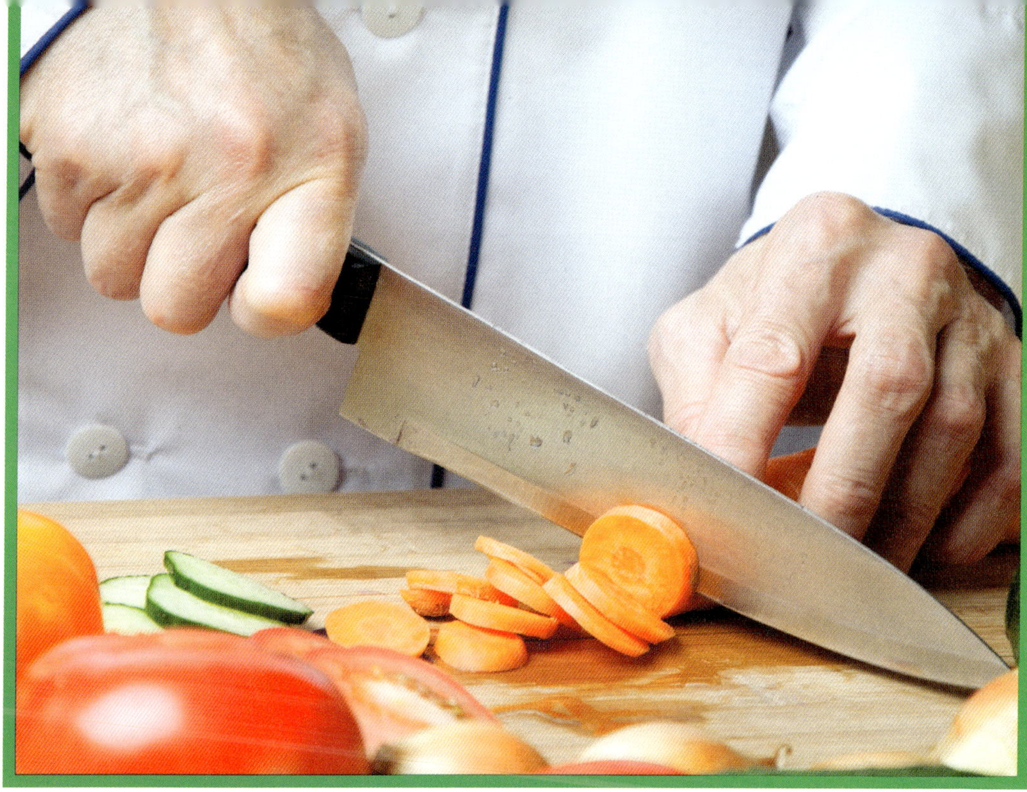

Dad has a 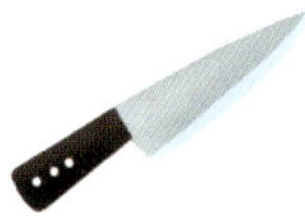 knife .

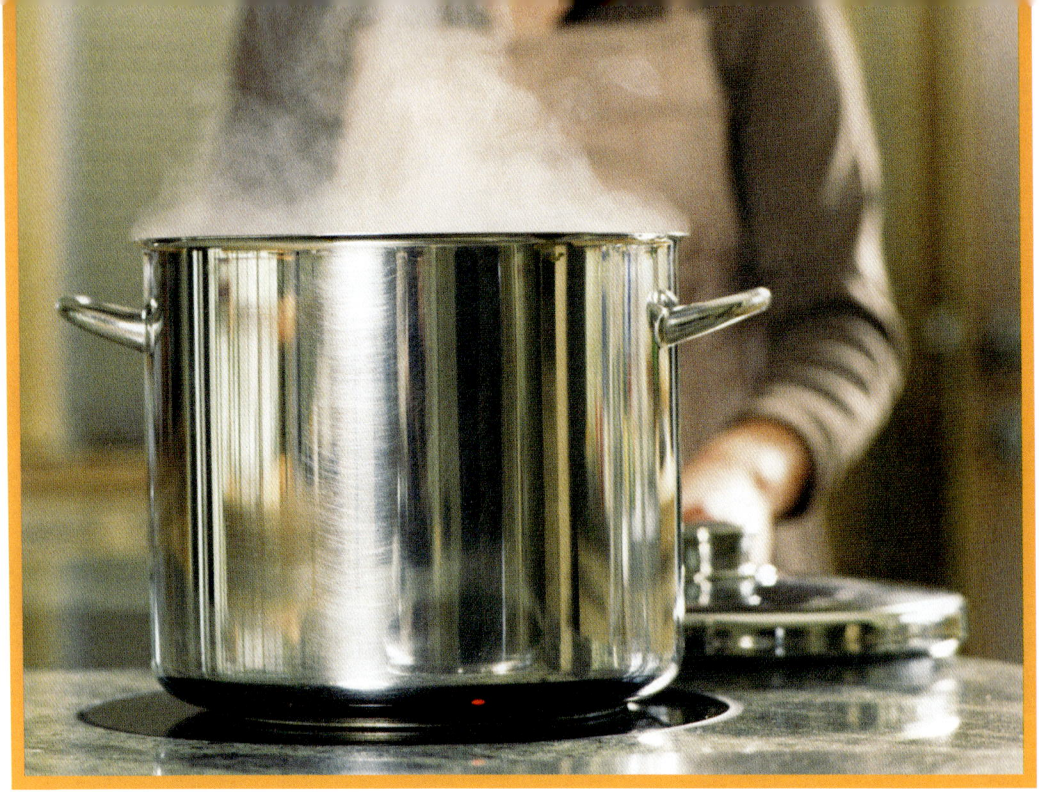

Dad has a 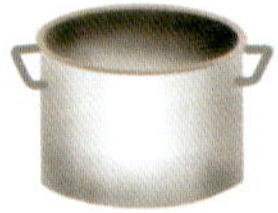 pot .

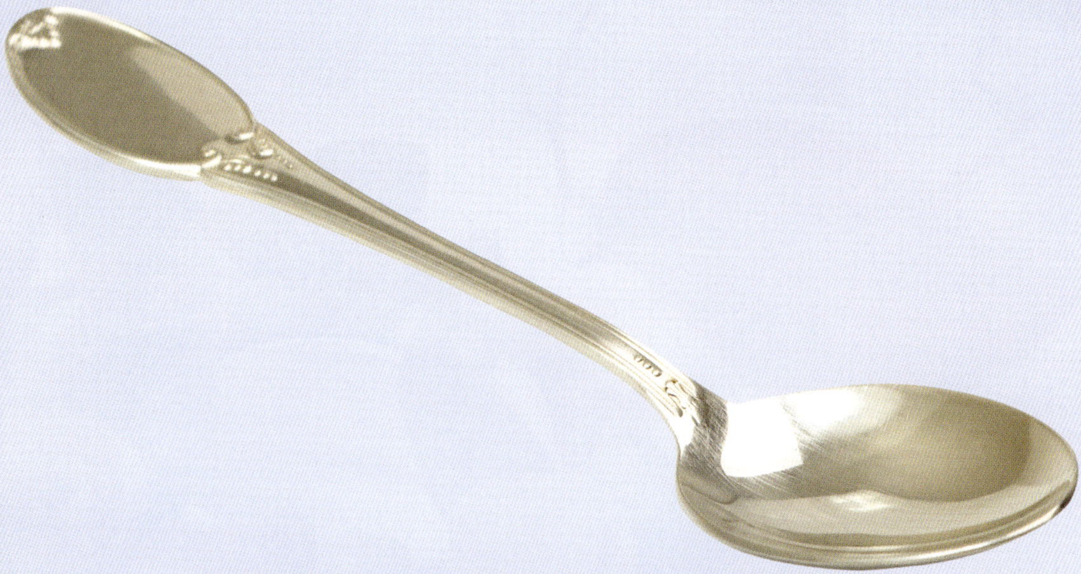

Dad has a 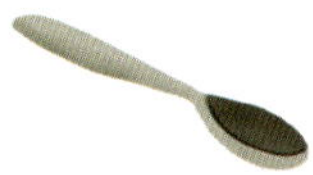 spoon .

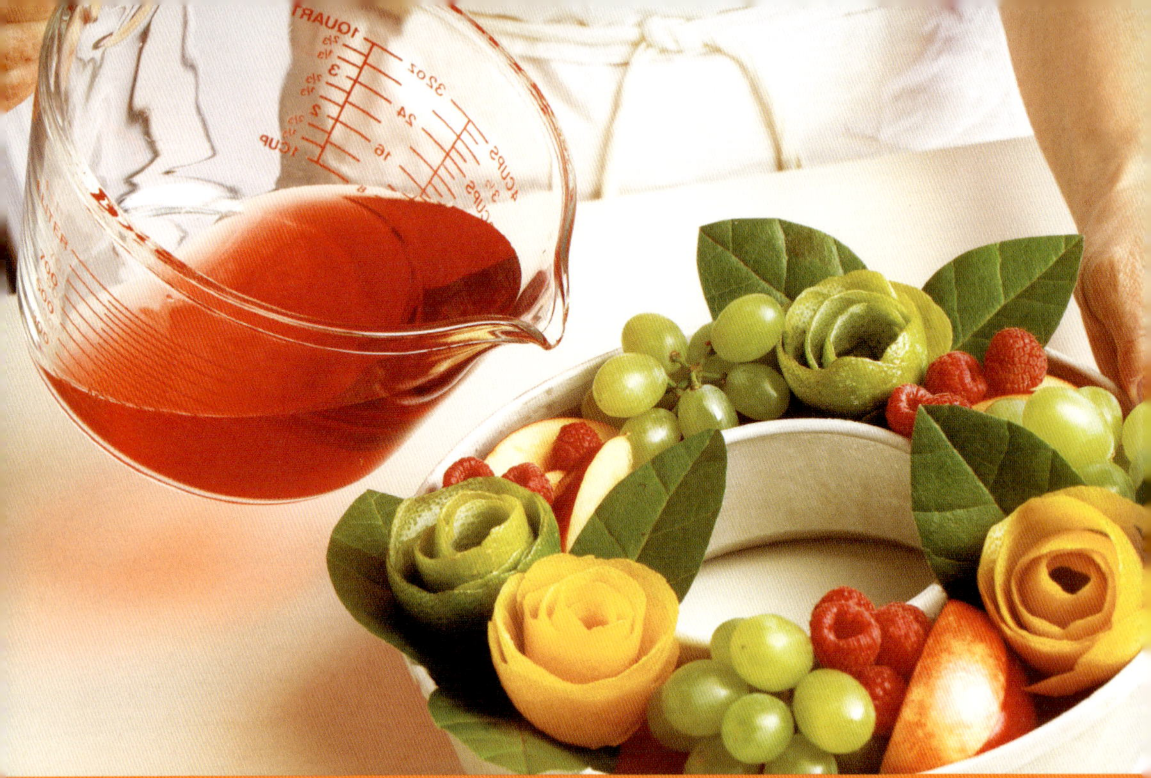

Dad has a 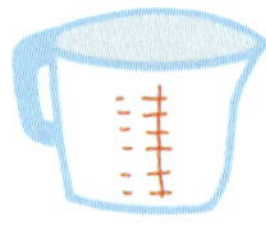 .

cup

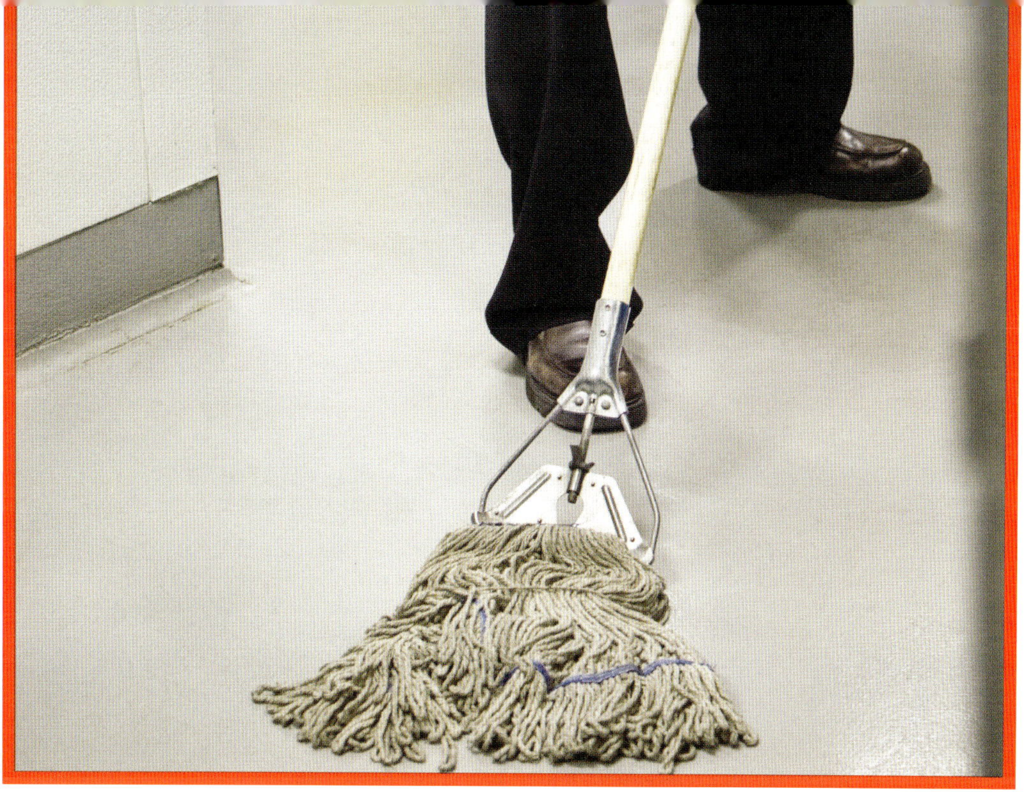

Dad has a 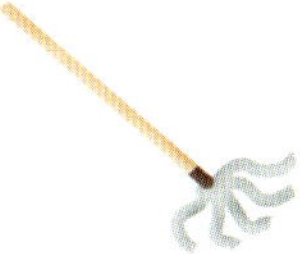 mop.

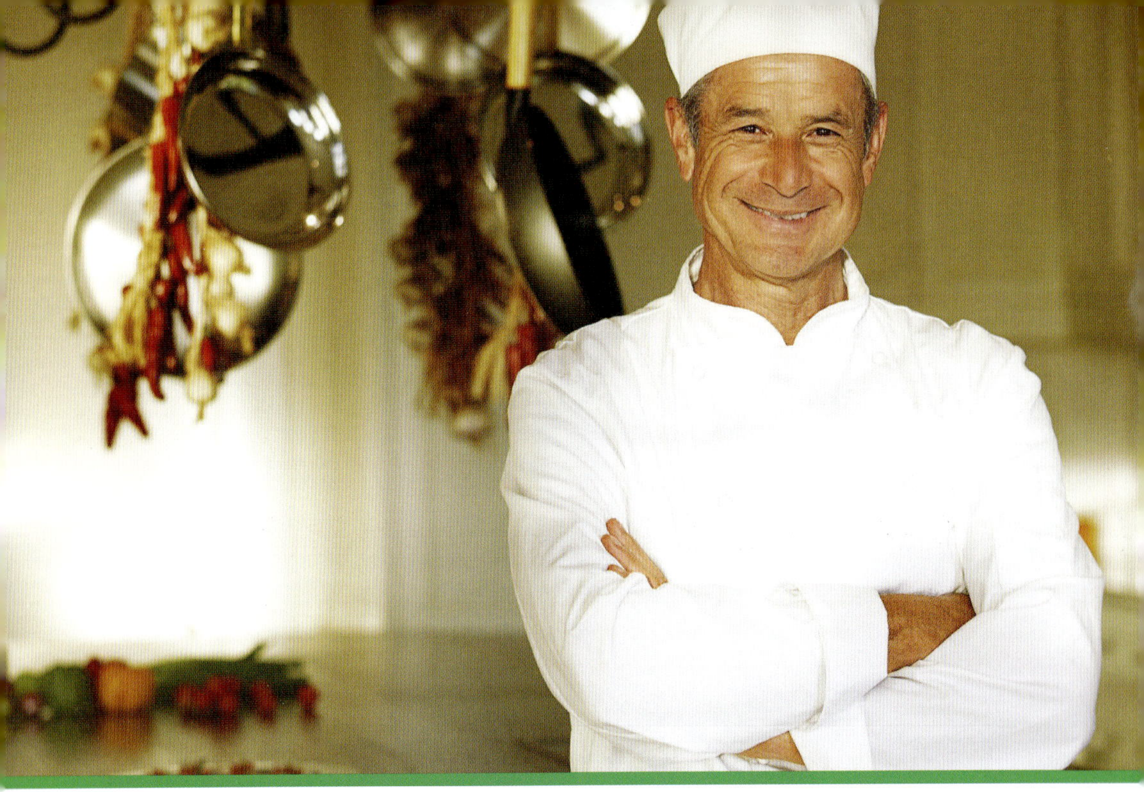

Dad is a 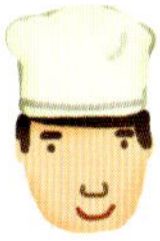 cook.